What Can I Make Today?

I Can Make a
Mask

Joanna Issa

Heinemann
LIBRARY

Chicago, Illinois

Edited by Penny West
Designed by Philippa Jenkins
Picture research by Elizabeth Alexander
Originated by Capstone Global Library Ltd
Production by Victoria Fitzgerald
Printed and bound in China by Leo Paper Group

18 17 16 15 14
10 9 8 7 6 5 4 3 2 1

Library of Congress Cataloging-in-Publication Data
Issa, Joanna, author.
  I can make a mask / Joanna Issa.
      pages cm.—(What can I make today?)
  Summary: "Using simple text and step-by-step instructions alongside clear, labeled photographs, this book shows how to make a selection of different bird masks"—Provided by publisher.
  Includes bibliographical references and index.
  ISBN 978-1-4846-0461-8 (hb)
  1. Mask making—Juvenile literature. 2. Masks—Juvenile literature. 3. Handicraft—Juvenile literature. I. Title.

TT898.I87 2015
731.75—dc23   2013039811

Acknowledgments
We would like to thank Capstone Publishers/ © Karon Dubke for permission to reproduce photographs.

Cover photograph reproduced with permission of Capstone Publishers/ © Karon Dubke.

We would like to thank Philippa Jenkins and Elizabeth Alexander for their invaluable help in the preparation of this book.

Every effort has been made to contact copyright holders of any material reproduced in this book. Any omissions will be rectified in subsequent printings if notice is given to the publisher.

Disclaimer
All the Internet addresses (URLs) given in this book were valid at the time of going to press. However, due to the dynamic nature of the Internet, some addresses may have changed, or sites may have changed or ceased to exist since publication. While the author and publisher regret any inconvenience this may cause readers, no responsibility for any such changes can be accepted by either the author or the publisher.

Contents

Some words are shown in bold, like this. You can find them in the glossary on page 23.

What Do I Need to Make a Mask?

To make the bird mask, you will need the head, beak, and eye templates, card stock, paper, a pencil, scissors, tape, a **brad**, and **elastic**.

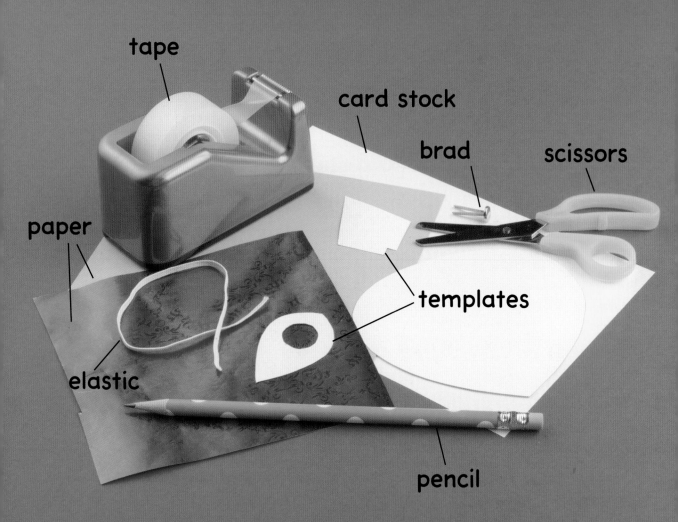

tape

card stock

brad

scissors

paper

templates

elastic

pencil

To make the templates, photocopy pages 21 and 22, and then cut out each shape.

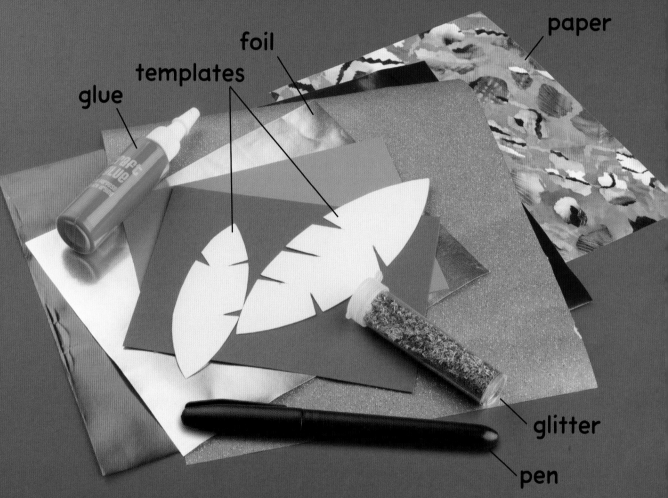

glue

templates

foil

paper

glitter

pen

To make the feathers, you will need the feather templates, paper, **foil**, a pen, glitter, and glue.

Make the Head

Put the head template on the card stock and draw around it. Then cut out the head.

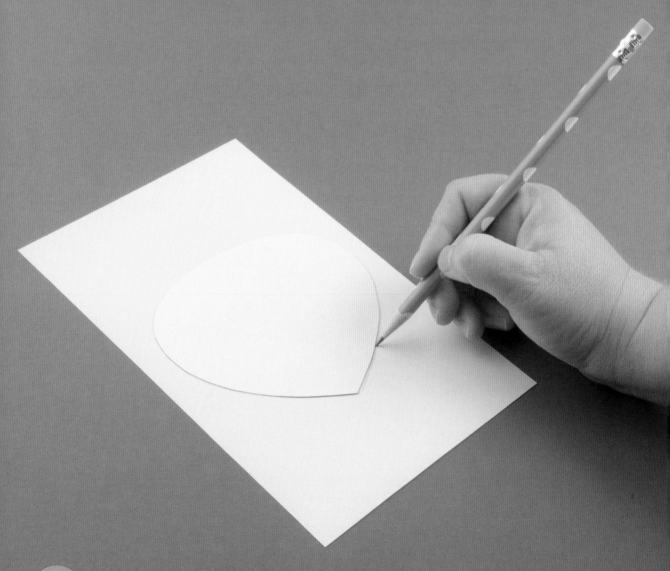

Make the Eyes

Put the eye template on some paper and draw around it twice to make two eyes.

Ask an adult to help you draw
eyeholes on the eye shapes and the
head. Then cut them out.

Make the Beak

Put the beak template on some paper and draw around it. Cut out the beak. Fold it down the middle to make a pointy end.

Make the Feathers

Put the big feather template on some paper or **foil**. Draw around it six times to make six feathers.

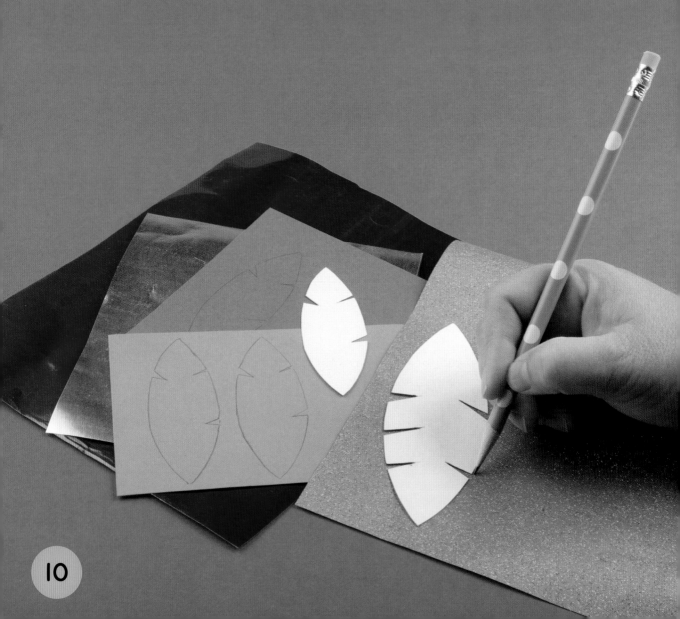

Put the small feather template on some paper or foil. Draw around it three times to make three feathers. Cut out your feathers.

Cut out shapes from colorful paper and **foil** to **decorate** your feathers.

You could also paint them or add glitter.

Decorate the Mask

Glue the feathers, eyes, and the beak onto your mask.

Make a line of dots around the eyes with a pen or with glitter.

Make two holes in the sides of the mask with a **brad**. Push **elastic** through the holes and tape it down.

Ask for **adult help**

Make an Owl Mask

Use the templates on pages 21 and 22 to make a different mask. Draw around the head template as before. Cut it out.

You can add large eyes to make an owl mask.

You can add different colored
feathers and a small beak.

What Can You Make Today?

You could make a colorful bird mask for a party or just for a fun costume.

Mask Templates

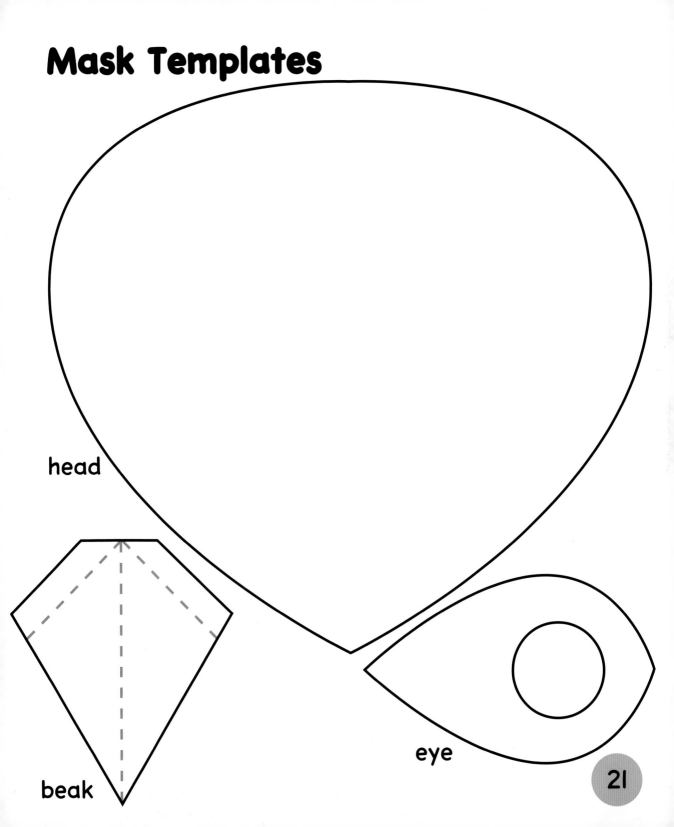

head

beak

eye

21

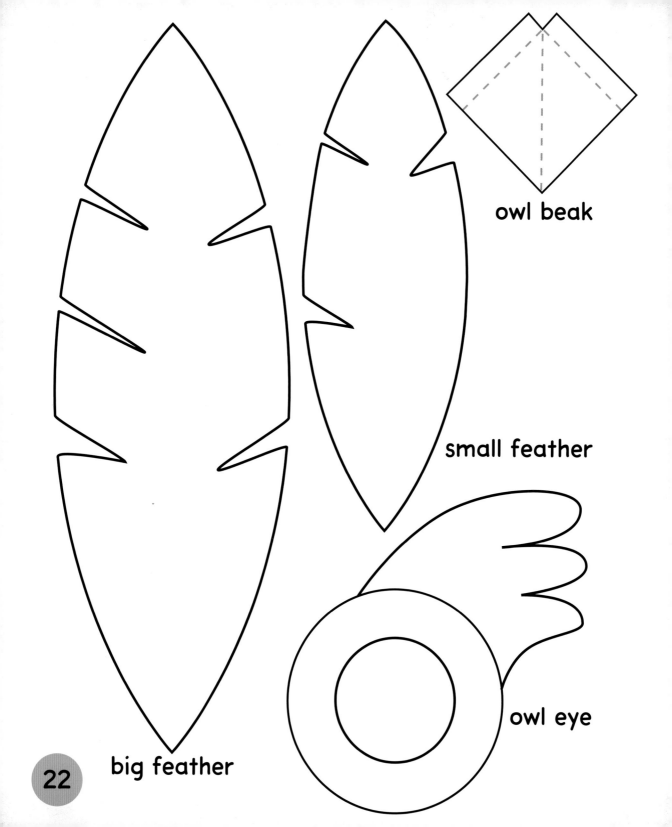

owl beak

small feather

owl eye

big feather

Picture Glossary

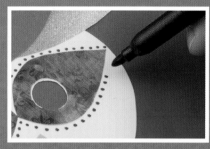 **decorate** add color or objects to make something interesting

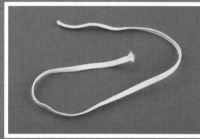 **elastic** thin fabric or cord that can be stretched

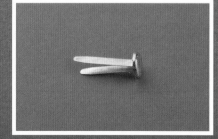 **foil** very thin metal sheets

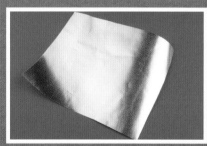 **brad** metal pin with ends that bend

Find Out More

Books

Henry, Sally, and Trevor Cook. *Making Masks.* New York: PowerKids Press, 2011.

Thomas, Isabel. *Masks and Face Painting* (Start with Art). Chicago: Raintree, 2011.

Web sites

Facthound offers a safe, fun way to find Internet sites related to this book. All of the sites on Facthound have been researched by our staff.

Here's all you do:

Visit www.facthound.com

Type in this code: 9781484604618

Index